"A runaway nun marries a university professor. Together they have six children and cause waves that change life across Europe and beyond. Gretchen Ronnevik captures the dynamic relationship of Katharina von Bora and her initially reluctant husband, Martin Luther, from its roots in her cloister experience to the end of their life together and the years of her widowhood with insight and sensitivity. This entertaining telling of the adventure that drove the Wittenberg Reformation brings to life Katie's vibrant personality, her sense of the gospel of Christ, and her skills at managing a household often bursting at the seams. A delightful, inspiring read for young and old."

    Robert Kolb, Professor of Systematic Theology
    Emeritus, Concordia Seminary

"As a pastor and father of five kids, I am so grateful for Gretchen Ronnevik's book about the life of Katie Luther. *The Story of Katie Luther* is much more than an excellent children's biography. As she tells Katie's story, Ronnevik teaches us about Reformation history, key theological concepts, and the freeing power of the gospel. This book is a wonderful resource for Christian parents and educators, making the riches of the Reformation accessible to young children."

    Adriel Sanchez, Pastor, North Park Presbyterian Church,
    San Diego, California; Host, *Core Christianity Radio*;
    author, *Praying with Jesus*

"In *The Story of Katie Luther*, Gretchen Ronnevik introduces readers to a pillar of the Reformation whose courage, intelligence, and trust in God make her well worth getting to know."
Lucy S. R. Austen, author, *Elisabeth Elliot: A Life*

"An utterly delightful tale of one of the Reformation's unsung heroines!"
Jared C. Wilson, Author in Residence, Midwestern Seminary; author, *Echo Island* and *The Storied Life*

The Story of Katie Luther

Lives of Faith and Grace

Edited by Champ Thornton

The Story of Katie Luther: The Nun Who Escaped to True Freedom

The Story of Martin Luther: The Monk Who Changed the World

The Story of Katie Luther

The Nun Who Escaped to True Freedom

Gretchen Ronnevik

WHEATON, ILLINOIS

The Story of Katie Luther: The Nun Who Escaped to True Freedom
© 2024 by Gretchen Ronnevik
Illustrations © Crossway
Published by Crossway
        1300 Crescent Street
        Wheaton, Illinois 60187

All rights reserved. No part of this publication may be reproduced, stored in a retrieval system, or transmitted in any form by any means, electronic, mechanical, photocopy, recording, or otherwise, without the prior permission of the publisher, except as provided for by USA copyright law. Crossway® is a registered trademark in the United States of America.

Cover and interior illustrations: T. Lively Fluharty

First printing 2024

Printed in the United States of America

Scripture quotations are from the ESV® Bible (The Holy Bible, English Standard Version®), © 2001 by Crossway, a publishing ministry of Good News Publishers. Used by permission. All rights reserved. The ESV text may not be quoted in any publication made available to the public by a Creative Commons license. The ESV may not be translated in whole or in part into any other language.

All emphases in Scripture quotations have been added by the author.

Trade paperback ISBN: 978-1-4335-9271-3

ePub ISBN: 978-1-4335-9273-7

PDF ISBN: 978-1-4335-9272-0

Library of Congress Cataloging-in-Publication Data

Names: Ronnevik, Gretchen, 1981- author.
Title: The Story of Katie Luther : the Nun Who Escaped to True Freedom / Gretchen
    Ronnevik.
Description: Wheaton, Illinois : Crossway, [2024] | Series: Lives of faith and grace |
    Includes bibliographical references. | Audience: Ages 8-13
Identifiers: LCCN 2023042433 (print) | LCCN 2023042434 (ebook) | ISBN
    9781433592713 (trade paperback) | ISBN 9781433592720 (pdf) | ISBN 9781433592737
    (epub)
Subjects: LCSH: Luther, Katharina von Bora, 1499-1552--Juvenile literature. |
    Reformation--Germany--Biography--Juvenile literature.
Classification: LCC BR328 .R66 2024 (print) | LCC BR328 (ebook) | DDC 284.1092
    [B]--dc23/eng/20240327
LC record available at https://lccn.loc.gov/2023042433
LC ebook record available at https://lccn.loc.gov/2023042434

Crossway is a publishing ministry of Good News Publishers.

V P			33	32	31	30	29	28	27	26	25	24
15	14	13	12	11	10	9	8	7	6	5	4	3	2	1

To Knut

Love,
Your Kette

"So if the Son sets you free, you will be free indeed."

JOHN 8:36

Contents

1 The Escape (1523)   *1*

2 A Life without Freedom (1504–1515)   *9*

3 Life as a Nun (1515–1523)   *21*

4 Reformation Rumblings (1505–1523)   *31*

5 Falling in Love (1523–1525)   *43*

6 Marriage before Love (1525)   *53*

7 An Unusual Marriage (1525–1546)   *63*

8 Blessing of Children (1526–1552)   *75*

9 Loss upon Loss (1527–1542)   *87*

10 An Open Home (1525–1546)   *97*

11 The Aftermath (1546)   *103*

12 War in Wittenberg (1546–1552)   *115*

    Conclusion: Lessons from a Life   *125*

    Study Questions   *129*
    Timeline   *137*
    More to Explore   *141*

1

The Escape

1523

EARLY EASTER MORNING, before sunrise, Katharina von Bora (*kah-tah-REE-nah von BOH-rah*) wrapped a shawl around her thin wool dress. It was chilly, but there was no frost that night. Without a sound, she walked softly and carefully down the hallway, along with a dozen or so other nuns. They did not say a word to each other, but exchanged glances full of terror and excitement. They were escaping.

As they reached the courtyard, they motioned to each other using hand signals to communicate so no one even had to whisper. Once outside, they heard a horse shaking his head, as his owner tried to keep him quiet and calm. Behind the horse was a cart that usually carried groceries or supplies. This was their way out.

The women climbed into the cart, and the man, Mr. Koppe, pulled a tarp over them to hide them from view. He flicked the reins, and the horse started walking across the courtyard, toward their gateway to freedom. As the pre-dawn sky began to turn from black to gray, these nuns made history. In the midst of the Protestant Reformation, these were the first nuns who dared to escape to freedom.

Escaping a cloister was dangerous. If they were caught, punishment could have been the death penalty. But for these nuns, this Easter Sunday, April 5, 1523, was about life not death. How fitting

THE ESCAPE

that on this Resurrection Day, they claimed their glorious new life of freedom in Christ!

But the decision to escape on Easter wasn't just fitting. It was smart. On this night the whole schedule of the cloister was different. All the nuns had stayed up the entire night for special services. That meant they were distracted and extra tired during this pre-dawn escape, and even the caretakers had extra duties.

Before this group of nuns slipped out, they had heard the Bible read, from Exodus 13–14. What better night to once again hear how Moses and all the Israelites had fled the slavery of Egypt! And how they, like the Israelites, were to be silent and make their escape:

> And Moses said to the people, "Fear not, stand firm, and see the salvation of the LORD, which he will work for you today. For the Egyptians whom you see today, you shall never see again. The LORD will fight for you, and *you have only to be silent*." (Ex. 14:13–14)

Tonight was the perfect night to escape. They had to go; so much had changed in the past few years. What they had learned meant they could not stay. Their home, the cloister, was a place to try to live a holy life, a life devoted to God and separate from the world.

Yet, their whole lives, the nuns had been told that they must try to attain perfection so that God would

— In Other Words —

A **cloister** is a home for a group of nuns or monks that is walled off and separate from the rest of society. Sometimes the place where nuns lived is also called a *convent*.

Indulgences were a practice by which people could pay money to the church to remove the consequences of their sins or their relatives' sins.

The **Protestant Reformation** was a movement in the 1500s to deal with corruption within the church. It ended up in a church split resulting in

THE ESCAPE

look kindly on them. The more perfect they were, the more God would hear their prayers. And because their prayers were supposed to be extra holy, people paid the church money to have nuns pray for them.

But recently there had been whispers among the nuns. Rumors swirled about the teaching of a monk. (Nuns were women, and monks were men.) His name

those who protested the corruption (Protestants) splitting off from the Roman Catholic Church, which was led by a man called the pope. This Reformation was led by Martin Luther.

Grace describes the forgiveness that God gives us, because of who he is, not because of what we have done or earned. God chooses to love and forgive because he is a loving and forgiving God, not because we have done things to make him love and forgive us. When God chases down sinners for the purpose of loving, forgiving, and freeing them from the trap of sin—this is grace.

KATIE LUTHER

THE ESCAPE

was Martin Luther, and he had questioned all this teaching about needing perfection and money to earn God's love. He had even challenged the pope!

And even after this monk had been kicked out of the church, he kept writing and teaching. His papers were passed around and discussed. They were so revolutionary! He said that God forgives us because of Christ's death and resurrection not because of what we do or don't do. In 1520, he published *The Freedom of the Christian*. He also started to publish writings specifically about the freedom of monks and nuns.

Martin Luther said that if any monk or nun had been forced *against his or her will* to take vows of obedience, poverty, and chastity, he or she was released from those vows. He said God wanted all Christians to live in freedom and that Christ's death on the cross paid for their freedom, not their money or good works. They couldn't earn grace. God didn't love monks or nuns more because they prayed several times a day, woke up throughout the night to pray, or because they took shelter from the world inside a cloister. Instead, they were free because of Jesus's death and resurrection, and this freedom was given freely through faith in Jesus. Life in the cloister wasn't a life of freedom; it was like a prison.

And now Katharina von Bora and her friends were escaping. But what lay ahead of them?

People all over the empire wondered: Was Martin Luther encouraging nuns to *not* pray several times a day and to *not* dedicate their lives to holiness? Was he actually encouraging a life of sin? What exactly did this "freedom of the Christian" mean practically?

On this Easter Sunday, Katharina von Bora was about to find out. It was Resurrection Day. It was the day her new life of freedom began.

2

A Life without Freedom

1504–1515

KATHARINA VON BORA had not always lived in a cloister. She was born in 1499 near Lippendorf, Germany, but when she was just five years old, tragedy struck. Her mother died, leaving her, her brothers, and possibly a sister in her father's care. Her father remarried right away, and her new stepmother brought more children into the household. There simply wasn't room for little Katie anymore.

Her father brought her to live at a cloister where she could go to school. It was a boarding school for girls

— Welcome to Katie's World —

What we call "Germany" today was a patchwork of independent states and territories that were part of the bigger "Holy Roman Empire" back in the 1500s. The Holy Roman Empire included most of Europe. Each territory in the empire would send an "elector" (often like a governor or prince) to a group called the "Electoral College" to vote on an emperor. However, the emperor also had to be crowned by the pope, who was the head of the worldwide church.

The emperor and pope had an agreement. The pope and the emperor each had their own powerful armies. There were the emperor's laws, and then there were the pope's laws called "canon law." The

A LIFE WITHOUT FREEDOM

from privileged families. They could get an education there, whether or not they ended up becoming nuns.

Katie's father owned land; he was a nobleman. (The *von* in Katharina von Bora's name means that

emperor ruled over the "secular" and the pope ruled over the "sacred."

Sacred/Canon Law was a set of rules that the church made and the church enforced on all Christians, no matter where they lived. The pope had his own courts, judges, army, and everything to enforce canon law.

Secular Law was a set of rules that the emperor made for the people in his empire, or rules that each elector or prince inside the Holy Roman Empire made for his lands. These rules had their own courts, judges, and armies as well.

People had to obey both secular and canon laws, even if sometimes they were different!

her father owned land, most likely given to him because he was a knight for a local prince.) But Katie's father wasn't very rich. While not many girls got an education in these days, Katie's father spent what little money he had to give her an education. He decided that Katie would live at the school where the nuns would raise her and teach her, along with the daughters of other noblemen.

So when she was only kindergarten age and still grieving the death of her mother, her father took her to the school located in the town of Brehna, Germany. She never went home again.

Life at the cloister in Brehna was strict and yet beautiful. The school had white stone archways that pointed to the heavens, and everything her eyes saw seemed clean and bright. She received a good education at Brehna. The nuns taught her how to read, how to write, and how to pray. Katie not only studied her native German language but also learned Latin, which was the language the church used for worship and study.

— Law and Order —

The cloister school in Brehna was part of the Benedictine Order. Benedict, who lived in the sixth century, wrote a rulebook called *The Rule of Saint Benedict* for monks and nuns who followed him. He taught about living a balanced life, separate from the world, so people could work on virtues like being humble, patient, and obedient.

Over time, the Benedictine convents all over the world started to have their own twists on the Benedictine Order. In the eleventh century, a group of Benedictine monks gave a name to their version of following the Benedictine Order: the Cistercian Order. The Cistercians wanted to follow *The Rule of Saint Benedict* the most, do it the best, and take the most extreme understanding of the rules. They even added to the rules, if they thought Benedict hadn't gone far enough.

Katie also made a few friends at the school, and they took care of each other. But there wasn't much time for fun. They had no choice but to work hard and study well, because there were severe punishments for misbehavior or laziness.

The entire cloister followed what was known as *The Rule of Saint Benedict*, which was basically the community rules, written by a monk hundreds of years earlier, about how to behave, how to think, and how to pray. So although she was not a nun, Katie and the other girls went to chapel services several times a day with the nuns, and learned to sing the Psalms in Latin.

As the seasons turned into years and Katie grew taller, the girls at the cloister became like sisters and the nuns like their mothers. They became her family.

Then one day, when she was ten years old, Katie's father sent a letter to the cloister. Something had happened to all his money, and he could no longer pay the small fee for Katie to live at the beautiful school. He would take her to a different cloister, with different nuns, and different girls. In a sense, she would be leaving her family again, her new Brehna family of nuns and school friends.

The new home was a cloister for poorer girls. And when she was old enough, Katie would also have to become a nun and live there for the rest of her life. If she became a nun, her father wouldn't have to keep paying every year for her food and shelter. At least she could be safe and provided necessities for her whole life.

It was a slow, hundred-mile cart ride to the convent in Nimbschen with her father. He shared news from home, and told Katie that she had family members who already lived at this new cloister. Her aunt Magdelene, her mother's sister, was a nun there, and the abbess (the woman in charge) was also related to her mother.

That long ride was the last Katie would see of the outside world for fourteen years. Her new home was not made out of white carved stone but large, round, gray field rocks. And the building wasn't grand and

GERMAN CITY PRONUNCIATION

Augsburg: OWGZ-boork
Braunschweig: BROWNSH-vyg
Brehna: Bre-NA
Lippendorf: lip-PEN-dorf

Magdeburg: MAHK-duh-boork
Nimbschen: NIMB-shen
Nüremberg: NYOOR-uhm-berg
Torgau: TORG-ow

Wittenberg: VIT-ten-berg
Zuhlsdorf: ZOOLS-dorf

Germany's borders have changed since Katie's day. This map shows Germany's present-day borders.

lofty but dark and cold. It was tucked in a little valley, far away from any town.

Though she did not know anyone there, Katie soon met her aunt Magdelene who ran the cloister's infirmary (like a hospital or clinic). Magdelene let her help in the infirmary. Katie learned how to bandage wounds and care for the nuns when they were sick. There was no school at this cloister, so she and a few other young girls learned how to be nuns by watching and imitating the older nuns who lived there.

Their lives were supposed to be separate from the world so that they could be "holy." (The word *holy* means "separate.") So they kept a distance from everything outside the walls of the cloister. They grew most of their own food, and if they needed anything else, the abbess would order extra supplies or groceries and have them quietly delivered without interaction. Even their gardens were surrounded by high walls, so that you couldn't see the rolling hills and farms around their home. The nuns were locked up in walls of the cloister, and there were caretakers who guarded their home to make sure no one got in and no one got out.

This "holiness" was taken to such an extreme that the nuns were separate not just from the world, but also separate from the rest of the church. Next to the cloister was a chapel, where only the nuns went to church. Inside the chapel there was a metal screen separating the nuns from anyone, like a farmer or tradesman, who might accidentally walk in. The nuns were supposed to stay separate from the rest of the world, so they could be "holy" and God would hear their prayers.

The nuns were even separated from each other! They weren't allowed to talk with each other, but just use their voices for prayer, singing, and confession. The abbess made sure the rules were followed. She also instructed the nuns about what was good and disciplined them when she thought they were bad.

As a result, people thought that because nuns were so pure and so separate, their prayers would have

A LIFE WITHOUT FREEDOM

more power. It was a nun's job to try to be as perfect as possible so her prayers would be heard by God.

For five years, Katie lived at the Nimbschen cloister, until she became old enough to start the formal process to become a nun. She felt trapped. What other options did she have? How else could she eat or live? Women couldn't just get a job back then. They weren't allowed to buy or rent property to live on without the permission of their father, husband, or brother.

It took a year of preparation and training to become a nun. And then at the age of sixteen, Katie took her vows and became a nun. Without her family to support her or another way to earn money, Katie had no other options.

It would take several more years before Katie would have a chance to escape this lonely life as a nun.

3

Life as a Nun
1515–1523

KATIE'S EYES OPENED as she heard the bell, waking up all the nuns. The sun was not yet up, but she took a deep breath, yawned, and then quickly got up and knelt next to her bed in the dark for morning prayers. She then smoothed out the clothes she had slept in, and put on her head covering, hoping it was straight. (Nuns were not allowed mirrors.) She then hurried out to the hallway, her head down, her hands cupped together, and she silently joined the stream of women walking to chapel. She'd have to work hard to stay awake.

As a nun, Katie was always tired. Nuns and monks weren't supposed to ever feel satisfied or comfort in worldly things. They weren't supposed to feel satisfied by a good night's sleep, a full stomach, comfortable clothes, or even close friendships. They were supposed to only feel satisfied in God. She was part of a Cistercian Order, which meant that it was one of the strictest kinds of Benedictine Orders. Every rule of Benedict was taken to the extreme so they could have the purest kind of virtue.

This was hard for Katie. She had such big feelings yet she felt like she had nowhere to put them. Following the rulebook felt like every part of her was being chipped away bit by bit until none of her was left. Each rule limited her freedom to make basic choices or even dream of something different. It was never

LIFE AS A NUN

a choice to become a nun, and yet she tried to make the best of it. And that meant trying to keep the three vows of obedience, poverty, and chastity.

The *vow of obedience* demanded that she had to obey God and also whatever her abbess told her. The abbess was the woman in charge of a cloister. Though Katie's abbess was a kind woman, and extra kind to her because they were related, she had absolute authority over all the women there. If you didn't do what she said, she could punish you however she liked.

And obedience was required in all things, no matter what, without question. That meant Katie had to do the chores she was commanded to do, only go to the outhouse when she was allowed to go to the outhouse, eat when they said she could eat, only eat the things they said she could eat, and only think the thoughts she was allowed to think. She had no say in any of it.

The *vow of poverty* meant that she couldn't own anything, ever. She could not keep trinkets, dolls, letters, jewelry, or anything—even if it was sentimental or from her family. She gave all she had to the cloister, and they would use it or give it to the poor. Anything that held memories of her family or her friends at her old school had to be given up.

Even clothing was limited. Katie was given an undyed white wool dress to wear, with a black apron, and black veil to cover her hair, and one extra set of clothes for wash days. She had to sleep in her

LIFE AS A NUN

clothes to be ready for prayer services at all times. And food was plain and sparse too. Being hungry was supposed to help the nuns' prayers. So no one was allowed meat, unless she was sick and needed to regain health.

The *vow of chastity* (meaning purity) meant that she could never get married or be with a man. Marriage provided a kind of loving satisfaction that was forbidden to nuns. The goal was to only feel satisfied with God.

Since the main job of a nun was to pray, the church wanted them to power up their prayers. One way that nuns were taught to "super-charge" their prayers was through using relics. Relics were objects that people thought had religious significance, almost like magical powers. Katie's cloister, along many others, had a huge collection of relics to help them in their prayers. These relics had been donated and put in gold-covered, and sometimes jewel-covered, chests.

Rich people had donated these expensive boxes to the cloister, often in exchange for indulgences.

And each indulgence, it was thought, could help people after death. At this time, the church believed not just in heaven and hell, but a third place called *purgatory*.

The church taught that purgatory was an in-between place for people who were sort of good and not totally evil. It was a place where people went after death. There, they endured some suffering to be purified for heaven. Although the Bible never mentions purgatory, the Roman Catholic Church said that if you buy indulgences, your time in purgatory would be shortened, and you'd get to heaven faster.

As a way for the church to make money, church officials said you could buy indulgences for your relatives who had died, so they could have shortened time in purgatory. When people were grieving the death of a loved one, they often worried about their loved one suffering in purgatory. People would donate their most valuable things to the church, thinking they were buying a faster way out of purgatory for their dead relatives.

LIFE AS A NUN

So the church got money from some people and relics from others. Then the nuns would use the relics to help bolster their prayers. They would kneel down in front of the ornate boxes, trying to super-charge their faith as they prayed and hoping all their efforts would make God more likely to answer their requests.

And they prayed *all* the time. Katie and the rest of the nuns got up at midnight, 3 a.m., and 6 a.m.

— Super-Charged Prayers —

Though real gold and jewels covered the relic boxes, there was no way to know about the religious objects inside. One box contained slivers of wood that someone claimed came from the manger Jesus was laid in as a baby. They also had a box with splinters of wood that were supposedly taken from the cross of the thief next to Jesus. There was another relic box with hairs in it that maybe came from Mary's head. And yet another relic box held thorns that someone said were from Jesus's crown of thorns.

KATIE LUTHER

for services where they prayed, sang, and read Scripture—all in Latin. She did chores too—all day long, cleaning, gardening, or helping in the infirmary. She and the others would also stop twice during the day for more prayers. They had one hour of rest after lunch, and then they went back to work, only to have an after dinner service at 6 p.m. Then they went to bed around 8 p.m., and started it all over again. There was little time for sleep (she never got more than three or four hours of sleep in one stretch) and even less time for friendship.

Sometimes Katie and another nun would smile at each other, and she would wonder if they would be friends if they were allowed to talk. Later, during confession, Katie would tell the abbess how she longed for friendship, and missed her school friends and family. As penance, the abbess would give her extra prayers to pray, so that she could be forgiven for wanting something that was not allowed.

Katie was tired. Yet she loved to pray. Hearing the voices of women fill the chapel in glorious harmony

LIFE AS A NUN

— A Day in a Cloister —

Daily Schedule of Services	
(including prayers, Scripture reading, and hymns)	
2:00 a.m.	Matins
5:00 a.m.	Lauds
Breakfast	
7:00 a.m.	Prime
9:00 a.m.	Terce
12:00 p.m. (noon)	Sext
An hour for rest	
3:00 p.m.	Nones
6:00 p.m.	Vespers
Supper	
9:00 p.m.	Compline
Bed	

The times are general as these times were set by the sun during the Middle Ages, and therefore fluctuated during the seasons. So this is just an idea of what it looked like on an average day.

We do not know for certain which chores Katie did and when those chores worked into the daily schedule. However, most people think she spent her time working in the infirmary.

was thrilling. Still no matter how much she worked, or how much she prayed, it never seemed to be enough. She wanted desperately to be satisfied in God, but it felt like God was never satisfied with her. The problem was that nothing she could do would make her holy enough.

Little did she know the solution was right around the corner. God had heard her prayers, and he had a surprise in store for Katie.

4

Reformation Rumblings
1505–1523

KATIE LIVED SHELTERED from the world around her. While she didn't know it at the time, the world was being turned upside-down by her future husband. Before they even knew each other, a monk, who lived over 70 miles away, changed Katie's life forever.

KATIE LUTHER

It went like this: in the year 1505, the same year Katie was being dropped off by her father at the cloister school, Martin Luther decided to not be a lawyer like his father wanted. Instead, he would become a monk, and devote his life to God. That same year, Pope Julius II, in charge of the whole church, made the decision to build a new church building in Rome: the Basilica of Saint Peter. It would be huge and expensive and beautiful. He wanted to fill it with exquisite artwork from Bramante, Raphael, and Michelangelo. This basilica was the enormous sanctuary the pope used personally, and he wanted the best of everything.

In order to pay for all the building and decorating, the pope needed to raise a lot of money. And that wasn't too hard, because sadly the church had become corrupt.

Many priests at this time did whatever they wanted, and the most powerful positions in the church like bishops or cardinals, were jobs that wealthy families would purchase for their sons so they could have money and power. For instance, the pope who came after him, Pope Leo X, came from the wealthy and corrupt Medici (*MEE-dee-chee*) family in Florence, Italy. And as greed for expensive things took over people in high positions in the church, the burden to produce the money for all these things fell on the common people.

The church made these regular people carry other burdens too. The church taught that Jesus died for sins, but his death was just to get the salvation process started. People learned that they had to do many other things to make salvation stick and to reduce their time in purgatory. People knew they were sinners and wanted to pay for their sins, and the corrupt church leaders were willing to take that payment— in cash. Powerful leaders were taking advantage of those with no power.

Martin Luther did not become a monk for power though. Trained as a lawyer, he wanted to follow God with his whole heart and obey all of God's laws. He chose to join an Augustinian order, which means that they used the rulebook taken from Augustine of Hippo. Unlike the rules of the Cistercians and Benedict that Katie's cloister followed, Augustine allowed monks to live in cities and to do things in the community like teach at a university. They didn't live as separately as the Benedictine orders.

Yet as Martin studied the law of God, he held himself to a higher standard than most monks and priests did, even in his more grace-filled order. Like Katie, no matter how much he tried, he couldn't

— Saintly Wisdom —

Augustine of Hippo was an ancient theologian who wrote a lot about the transforming grace of God. He lived in AD 354–430 in northern Africa. He is still considered one of the most influential theologians in the church, and his books like *Confessions* and *City of God* are still read and discussed today. He emphasized the sinful state of humans and our desperate need for the grace of God.

make himself perfect. He could not avoid needing God's grace, day after day.

Sometimes Martin would spend hours confessing all of his sins, and then on his way back to his room, he would think of more sins he had done and would run back to confession. He tried to discipline his body and mind, but no matter how disciplined he was, he knew it was not good enough—at least not good enough for God.

The priest who mentored Martin, named Dr. Johann von Staupitz, tried to encourage him. He would tell Martin to settle down; God was not as harsh as Martin imagined. But Martin knew God required perfection and that his life was far from perfect according to God's law.

Dr. Staupitz knew Martin needed to serve other people and not think about himself so much. Therefore he organized for Martin Luther, who was smart and disciplined, to be given the job of teaching theology at the university in Wittenberg, where Martin would teach future priests.

Martin moved into the cloister next door to the university. It was called the "Black Cloister" as all the monks living there wore long black robes. Martin also preached at the local church. Until then, sermons weren't a very common part of the church service. Common people simply went to church to get the Lord's Supper, called *mass*. But Martin Luther decided to start preaching verse by verse through Romans, Galatians, and Hebrews.

Studying these books in depth, Martin Luther started to understand the grace of God that was given through Christ alone. It wasn't for sale. It couldn't be earned. This is what he read in Galatians 2:21, "I do not nullify the grace of God, for if righteousness were through the law, then Christ died for no purpose." Grace is a gift from God.

So when a traveling salesman came through Wittenberg, sent by the pope to sell indulgences, Martin Luther knew it was a problem. God's grace and forgiveness weren't for sale! No one is purified by works or money or indulgences. People are purified by the

REFORMATION RUMBLINGS

KATIE LUTHER

blood of Christ. It couldn't be earned—it was a free gift. Martin Luther wanted to address the problem of indulgences. On October 31, 1517, he attached to the church door (the town's public bulletin board) his *Ninety-Five Theses*. This was basically a list of ninety-five statements that spoke out against indulgences and the manipulation of God's grace.

The first of these statements was "When our Lord and Master Jesus Christ said, 'Repent' (Matt. 4:17), he willed the entire life of believers to be one of repentance." To *repent* means "to turn." Martin Luther said that even our *good* works were tainted by pride or bad motives. The Christian life, then, wasn't looking to any of our works, but looking to Christ and Christ alone. It is a turning from depending on ourselves to depending on Christ.

These ninety-five statements caught the attention of the world, and everyone had questions.

The pope was not happy! The more people read Luther's statements, the less money they gave to the church for indulgences. The pope said he wanted to grow the church. But in order to form the church into the powerful empire as he envisioned it, he needed money and powerful people on his side. Martin Luther disagreed. The church was built on Christ

— Small Print, Big Business —

Johannes Gutenberg invented his printing press—with new moveable letters—around 1450. With this new technology, scribes no longer had to handwrite books or scrolls, and news was more easily spread all over the world. In 1454, the Roman Catholic Church started putting it to use by printing mass amounts of certificates called *indulgences* and selling them off to people for money. Then Martin Luther began using the printing press in 1517 to publish his writings and sermons that were distributed all over the empire. Through the rest of his life, he never took any money for his pamphlets and let the printers and distributors keep all of the profits.

alone. Salvation was by faith alone through grace alone. It could not be earned, and it was not for sale.

As a result of his writings, Martin Luther got death threats. But Martin had some powerful friends, who also thought the church had become corrupt. These friends protected him, and Martin could continue to write. And he wrote like he was going to war against anyone who would belittle the grace of God. Three years after he posted the *Ninety-Five Theses*, Martin wrote short booklets or pamphlets telling monks and nuns they couldn't earn their salvation and they couldn't earn holiness. It's a gift from God.

It was writings like these that, thanks to the technology of the printing press, likely made their way to Katie's cloister all the way in Nimbschen. The deliveryman who brought groceries to Katie's cloister was a good friend of Luther's.

Soon this powerful message of grace pulsated across Germany and around the world, and even through the thick walls of Katie's cloister. This was the message that gave her courage to leave a life

REFORMATION RUMBLINGS

— In His Own Words —
The Freedom of the Christian

One of Martin Luther's pamphlets was called *The Freedom of the Christian*. In it he wrote, "A Christian is completely free, subject to nothing and no one. A Christian is a dutiful servant, subject to everyone." This is what is called a *paradox*. It's when two things that seem to be opposite are true at the same time.

What Martin Luther meant by this was that Christ paid for all our sin—all of it. No one, not even the church, is allowed to put burdens on our salvation where Christ has put none. At the same time, now that we belong to God, we should use that freedom to serve and love our neighbors. God has called us to be servants in his name to those around us.

In this booklet, Martin Luther tried to explain good works weren't for earning God's love, they were for showing God's love.

KATIE LUTHER

where she was trying to be perfect so God would approve of her. Thanks to Martin Luther's writings, she discovered that God already approved of her because of what Christ had done for her. As a Christian she was free to love and serve her neighbors.

For Katie, this changed everything. But questions remained. If she wasn't earning God's love, if her prayers weren't extra special because of all of her good works, if she was truly free in Christ to love and serve her neighbors . . . then what was the benefit of being a nun? What was she doing staying there?

5

Falling in Love

1523–1525

KATIE AND THE OTHER NUNS climbed out of Mr. Koppe's wagon looking disheveled and tired. They had finally reached a safe territory where the local elector was friends with Martin Luther. The local pastor there in Torgau saw their messy hair and wrinkled clothes and wanted to help. So he arranged for the nuns to have a place to rest and something to eat. He gave them new clothes so they would blend in better for the rest of their journey to Wittenberg.

The next day, the group of nuns arrived at Martin Luther's doorstep. The Black Cloister had forty rooms that used to be monk bedrooms. Most of them were now empty. After Martin Luther proclaimed that monks could be free of their vows, almost all of them had left (except for one very old monk, who stayed at the cloister with Martin).

The local elector had told Martin Luther he could keep the old place, since he still worked at the local university next door. But as Martin was so busy, and the cloister was so empty, it didn't take long for dirt and cobwebs to overwhelm it. He had no time to take care of such a huge place. Still whenever someone needed a place to sleep, Martin let him stay there. Unfortunately, some of his guests would take things from the house, even things like the pots and pans. The cloister was becoming rundown in a hurry.

FALLING IN LOVE

But when the women arrived at Martin's doorstep, he believed it wouldn't be proper to just let a bunch of women stay at his house. The world was watching, as these were the first nuns who had dared to leave their vows. Still, he promised to take care of them. Martin Luther quickly sent messages to various families, asking if they would house the women and feed them for at least a week or two.

But this was only a short-term solution for the nuns. When monks left their vows, they were able to get new jobs; they were able to survive. But what about the nuns? There weren't many jobs available to women. Plus, in that country at that time, it was illegal for women to not have a male guardian in charge of them. Some of the nuns who escaped were able to go back to their families. The rest, like Katie, could not. In some cases, like Katie's, their families had no money to support them. In other cases, the families refused because they feared punishment from the church or the government for taking care of an escaped nun.

Martin Luther wanted to help but had no money to support all the remaining women. So he started playing matchmaker! He would host parties at the Black Cloister, and introduce former nuns to either former monks or nice students from the university. Martin wanted to see if he could get these women husbands, and therefore homes, fast.

— Legally Binding —

Just like children need an adult to look after them, so during this time, it was also the law for women to have a guardian as well. Without a guardian, women could not hold property, have a job, or get permission to marry. This is why nuns were much more resistant to leave their vows than monks. This unfortunate situation was also why, when Katie's group of nuns (who were the first ever to dare to leave their cloister) arrived at Martin Luther's cloister, it had been emptied of monks for well over a year.

FALLING IN LOVE

To Katie, all the parties at the Black Cloister, with dancing, music, and laughter were overwhelming—such a contrast to the silent life she had lived up to that point. Her body buzzed with the noise of it all. The families she was staying with showed her how to do her hair and how to dress properly, as these were things that were not considered important as a nun. They also taught her to dance and encouraged her.

Before long, Katie fell in love with a kind man named Jerome Baumgärtner. They started going on walks together, and they loved talking together. Dancing with him felt like magic. Katie felt like, for the first time, all of her dreams were coming true. All of their friends agreed it was a good match, and even Martin Luther thought they were perfect for each other. As things started getting serious, and when it seemed as though a proposal would be soon, Jerome went home to see his family in Nüremberg. He planned to ask his parents for permission to marry her. He intended to come back soon.

FALLING IN LOVE

Katie waited. She watched each of her friends get engaged and married, one by one. Weeks turned into months. To keep her from overstaying her welcome too long in one place, Martin Luther moved her from her first temporary home to the Cranach family. They were a well-connected noble family.

She became very close with the lady of the house, Barbara Cranach, who treated her like a daughter and showed her how to run a large household. While staying there, Katie also met many of their other house guests, including famous people, like King Christian III, the king of Denmark, Sweden, and Norway. He became her friend, and told her to write to him if she ever needed anything.

But still Katie waited for Jerome to return. It could not go on like this forever. Martin Luther worried Jerome was not coming back, so he tried setting up Katie with another man. Martin figured getting some competition going would get Jerome to come back. Martin wrote Jerome to say that Katie would soon be falling in love with someone else if he didn't hurry.

KATIE LUTHER

But Katie did not want to become engaged to someone else. Still, Martin Luther tried to match her up with a pastor named Dr. Caspar Glatz. He was no one's first choice. This man was stingy with his money, his words, and his compliments. He was cranky and argumentative. Katie didn't think she could handle marrying a man she could not respect. Her strong will flared, and she told Martin there was no way he could convince her to marry Dr. Glatz.

Katie refused to marry him, even though it made her life difficult. She was penniless and had no other options. But she had escaped for freedom not for another prison in the form of an unwanted marriage. And Katie's intuition about Dr. Glatz proved correct. Later on in his life, he was fired from his church for being too argumentative!

Before long, things became much more complicated for Katie. Her life had become entangled with the turbulent politics of the Reformation. The enemies of the Reformation wanted to see her fail, because if she who trusted Martin Luther failed to

FALLING IN LOVE

find a home and guardian, then other people might stop listening to Martin Luther. These enemies also wanted to make Katie miserable to send a message to any other nuns who might be thinking of escaping their cloisters.

And then, not just in Wittenberg, but all over the empire, people started to gossip. Because Katie had

— Witch Trials —

Some people even thought Katie might be a witch. This was dangerous gossip because witches were executed in those days. This was the beginning of the witch trials that happened all over Europe, and eventually in America. During Katie's lifetime in Wittenberg, four women were executed for being witches. People didn't know what to think about women—whose lives were supposed to be dedicated to God—leaving their imprisoned lives to live in freedom. Every move they made was watched with suspicion.

KATIE LUTHER

not yet married, people thought she must be stuck up or immoral for what looked like her desire to flirt with men. Then newspapers joined in. They kept printing about how undesirable, ugly, and sinful she was.

People who knew Katie knew all this gossip was all lies. But her reputation started to fall apart as people saw her as the runaway nun that no one wanted to marry.

She was in a terrible position. Still, Katie waited patiently for Jerome to return to her.

Finally, she heard that her love, Jerome, had married a very young, wealthy girl from a powerful family. Obviously, Jerome's family didn't like the idea of him marrying a runaway nun with no money.

Brokenhearted, Katie had to think of something fast.

6

Marriage before Love

1525

KATIE'S MIND WAS RACING. Who could she marry? She tried to picture every unmarried man she had met since her escape. That one was too silly, that one was too petty, that one argued too much, and that one was too young. She mentally crossed off each eligible man that came to mind.

Who could she live with? Who could she build a life with? He would have to be someone like-minded and honorable. Someone who kept his word. Someone who believed in the power of the gospel that Martin Luther had explained so well.

That was it—Martin Luther!

He was sixteen years older than she was, but that didn't bother her. She was sure she could help him in his work. He was obviously in over his head—just look at the state of his home! She could take some things off his plate and allow him to do what he did best: preach and write.

So she came up with a plan and went to Luther's friend, Nicolaus von Amsdorf (von AHMS-dorf). Katie told him that she was content to stay unmarried. Maybe no one would want her. But *if* she was going to get married, there were only two men she would ever accept: him (Nicolaus) or Martin Luther. They were the only two men she respected enough to marry. She could not marry someone she did not respect. Martin Luther had given his word that he

MARRIAGE BEFORE LOVE

would look after the nuns who had left the convent at Nimbschen. Now she was calling on him to keep his promise.

Nicolaus went to Martin Luther and delivered the news, and said Katie would only accept Martin Luther as a husband. (He must not have wanted to marry Katie either.) Martin didn't know what to do. He had no intention of marrying, and if he had wanted to marry, he said he'd probably have chosen Ava, one of the other nuns from Nimbschen. But he'd already married her off. Ava had a sweet, obedient spirit, and Katie was . . . well, Katie was strong-willed. She had strong opinions, spoke her mind, and she did what she thought was right, no matter what anyone thought about it.

Martin knew he was stubborn as well, so he worried they would just argue all the time if they got married. And he didn't have romantic feelings for Katie at all—but he did respect her. He respected her strong opinions, because in all fairness, they were usually the same as his. He respected that when she had read his words, she believed them so much that she left her life as a nun. She believed that theology meant something, not just in theory, but in real life.

So Martin talked to his closest friends about the idea. Most of them were against it. Taking on a wife would be a great distraction and burden while trying to do his work. He was already overwhelmed! But a few of his friends encouraged it, saying it would make a public statement that marriage for priests was good. (At this time, the church didn't allow priests to marry for many of the same reasons they didn't let monks or nuns marry.)

In his own mind, Martin debated back and forth. It would make a powerful theological statement for him to get married. But he had nothing to offer a wife. He had no money, and he was overworked. Not only that, but as a church Reformer, Luther's life was almost always in danger. Reformers before him had been burned at the stake. He didn't know how "safe" of a life he could offer Katie. He could easily be killed at any time. Who would be her guardian then?

MARRIAGE BEFORE LOVE

However, as Martin tried to decide what to do, another thought came to his mind. One of his greatest regrets was that he had initially become a monk against his father's wishes. He had not honored his father as he now thought he should have done. And his father had always wanted him to get married and have a family. So now that he was no longer a monk, maybe marrying Katie would honor his father and help mend his relationship with him.

In the end, Martin's decision came down to what he believed about Christian duty. He had given his word to Katie that he would care for her and find her a suitable husband. It was also his duty as a son to honor his father's wishes and get married. By marrying Katie, he reminded himself as he paced back and forth, he could keep his word, help someone in need, and honor his father's wishes. And what did the Bible teach? Martin strongly believed that if God brought someone into his life who needed his help, and he was able to help, he was obligated as a servant of Christ to help. Katie needed his help and his protection. When people asked why he married Katie, he said "to spite the devil," because the devil wouldn't want him helping others.

So with his mind made up, he went to Katie, and asked her to marry him.

In that time, it was thought that Tuesdays were a lucky day for weddings, so on Tuesday, June 13, 1525, Martin and Katie were married. Only five people

MARRIAGE BEFORE LOVE

witnessed their marriage, three of Luther's friends and Lucas and Barbara Cranach, who had taken care of Katie. (Luther's best friend, Philip Melanchthon (*mel-AHNK-tohn*), was excluded because he was against the marriage.)

Martin and Katie Luther were not "in love" on their wedding day. But they both had an enormous

respect for the other. They both were determined to serve the other with the riches of grace that they believed God had already given each of them.

Many people had wanted to be at the wedding of the famous Martin Luther and his bride, the runaway nun. So they decided to have a public ceremony and a wedding feast on June 27 where everyone was invited.

— Wedding Gifts —

Common wedding gifts around this time were cloth diapers (called swaddling cloths), cradles, or baby bathtubs. Though the Luthers might have received these, only the wealthiest gifts were recorded. Because both Martin and Katie had been living in poverty due to their previous monastic vows, all the princes and organizations associated with Martin Luther wanted to shower them with gifts to help start off their lives. Some of the recorded wedding gifts were 20 *guilden* (German money)

MARRIAGE BEFORE LOVE

There was no one as excited to be there as Luther's parents—his father was giddy that this day had finally come. Since Martin and Katie had both been under a vow of poverty for most of their lives, they had almost nothing. But their rich and powerful friends brought lavish gifts and even supplied them with beautiful wedding rings. It was a wonderful feast with all the best of everything.

and a barrel of Einbeck beer from the Wittenberg council, a large silver tankard (like a fancy cup or mug) from the University of Wittenberg, and a pair of wedding rings from Willibald Pirckheimer of Nüremberg. Luther's wedding band was a double ring with a diamond and ruby, with his and Katie's initials inscribed on the band, and inscribed on the inside were the words: WHAT GOD HAS JOINED TOGETHER NO ONE SHOULD SEPARATE. Katie's ring had a ruby with a crucifix on either side of the stone and inscribed on the inside were both her and Luther's names and their wedding date.

KATIE LUTHER

And the joy continued to grow. Luther had written to a friend on June 21 (in between the real wedding and the public wedding) that he was not passionately in love but he did love and esteem his wife. But by August 11, he was writing friends, saying Katie was perfect for him, and that he wouldn't trade her for all the treasure in the world! It did not take long at all for them to become completely devoted to each other.

When Katie moved into the Black Cloister as Martin's bride, it was not a pretty picture. Martin hadn't even cleaned his sheets in a year! When he got home from work each day at the university, he was so exhausted that he just fell into bed. Once the wedding feast was done, without any romantic honeymoon, Katie immediately got to work cleaning the place up. There was so much to do to make this unkempt cloister a home.

7
An Unusual Marriage
1525–1546

MARTIN LUTHER had been so overwhelmed by writing and preaching and teaching during the last few years that he didn't realize how much he was aching for help. Happily, Katie was eager to help and she was used to hard work from her days as a nun. Martin never needed to wonder what Katie thought about things, because she spoke her mind. And since she was so eager to get to work, he gave his wife complete control of the house. Martin told her it was her domain to rule over, as long as she didn't rule over him.

As she settled into her new life, Katie quickly realized that Martin was horrible in handling money. Because he was famous, people expected him to have money. And people expected Katie to have money because she was from a noble family. Neither was true.

He refused to accept any money earned from his writings, and even though he got a salary from the university where he taught, he gave the money away to whomever needed it. He also had an open hand with his possessions. He welcomed visitors into his home, the Black Cloister, and let them take whatever they wanted. So his home was in shambles, and it didn't appear generous, as he intended. It looked mismanaged.

When he gave control of the money over to Katie in their first year of marriage, she had every room in the Black Cloister scrubbed and disinfected. With

AN UNUSUAL MARRIAGE

money that was gifted to them at their wedding, she ordered two huge wagonloads of lime to whitewash the inside of those rooms. Now whenever Martin let people stay with them, the rooms were suitable for people to occupy. And for those who could afford it, Katie would now charge a small fee for living and eating there. By earning a little money, she could also hire some servants to keep the Black Cloister clean and fight diseases like the black death which seemed to come in waves to Wittenberg.

The next problem was food. Martin was always inviting students over to discuss theology over supper, but they had no food to serve their guests. Katie looked at the cloister's overgrown garden. It hadn't been touched since all the monks left years ago. So she started growing all sorts of vegetables in it. Within a year, it was overflowing with produce, and Martin and Katie were now able to offer fresh food for guests who wanted to eat at their table.

At first, Katie had one or two servants who helped her manage this huge cloister and all the people who

KATIE LUTHER

AN UNUSUAL MARRIAGE

stayed there. Eventually she had about twelve people working for her, running the whole place that was always buzzing with people. She was grateful for the practical knowledge for running a large household that she had acquired while living with the Cranachs.

Even though she had servants, Katie worked as hard as anyone else. She woke up at 4 a.m. every morning, before everyone else, to get the household started. Referring to the brightest object in the sky, that appeared right before sunrise, her husband started calling her the "morning star of Wittenberg."

Needing even more help, Katie wrote to her aunt Magdelene at the Nimbschen cloister. In the letter, Katie convinced her aunt to escape the cloister too! And soon her aunt Magdelene had moved in with Martin and Katie at the Black Cloister. She was a huge help to Katie, especially when it came to nursing the sick and using parts of the cloister as a hospital.

Then Katie started buying and breeding cows so that she could serve meat and milk to all of their guests. Before long she added pigs to her farm, and she leased a field for them to graze in. Soon she also started a brewery in an old building on the compound, because beer was considered the hospitable drink to serve.

Katie helped Martin manage money, but she never told him to stop being generous. On the contrary, she wanted him to give away whatever God put on his heart to give away or to help the people God brought before him to help. In fact, she enabled him to help others *more* through her careful management. However, sometimes she went behind his back and accepted gifts on his behalf that he didn't want to accept. (Sometimes she thought he was being rude in refusing, or she simply thought the gift could serve their household, as she knew what housing and feeding all those people cost.)

Though they didn't always agree on everything, Martin soon realized what a blessing Katie was to his ministry. She was not a burden. He continued to give her more and more oversight and control. He

AN UNUSUAL MARRIAGE

knew that whatever he gave her, she would return to him ten times better. It was as if everything she touched turned to gold. And her mind kept thinking up more things to do!

Most marriages back then weren't partnerships like this. The amount of control Martin gave to Katie caught people's attention. Several of the students from the school where Martin taught felt uncomfortable with the freedom given to Katie. Many of these students lived with them, and ate at the Luthers' table. After the meal, they'd take notes about what Martin said or how he and Katie talked to each other. They'd write about how bold she was and how he just let her be bold, often without correction.

Sometimes Martin would argue back with her. But most often, in Luther's sarcastic sense of humor, he would call her "My Lord Katie" to give her honor in a way that made his opponents uncomfortable. He gave her other nicknames like, "Boss of Zuhlsdorf" (Zuhlsdorf was a farm she later bought) or "Doctor Katharina." Or when she got too bossy with him, he called her "My *Kette*," which sounds like her name, but means "chain" in German.

Katie and Martin were both outspoken and strong-willed. But the secret to their love was that their strong wills were pointed in the same direction and rooted in the theology of Christian freedom. They had started their marriage with only respect and the love of Christ. And they continued to give each other as much freedom as the other needed. They believed that God was using them to love and serve each other.

Although the students who sat at the Luthers' table could see Martin and Katie's love up close, most people did not have such a clear view. Everyone wanted to hear the latest gossip about what the Luthers' marriage was really like.

Unfortunately, that meant the talk and gossip about Katie did not stop when she married Martin Luther. If anything, it increased. And now Katie attracted not just her own enemies, but also Martin's enemies as well. Martin was a huge celebrity, and the fact that he, a former monk, had married

AN UNUSUAL MARRIAGE

a former nun (neither of whom were supposed to marry) made many people very angry. They saw it as going against the church and all that was holy.

— Open to Debate —

Some of Luther's most famous writings, his letters to Erasmus, would not have been written without Katie. Erasmus was another famous theologian at the time who often attacked Luther's theology. Luther's friends told him he should write Erasmus back, debate him, and correct the false claims he was making about Martin Luther. When Martin's friends couldn't get him to respond to Erasmus, they went to Katie, and explained to her why his response was so important.

Katie asked him to respond to Erasmus's attacks, and Martin listened to her. When he didn't listen to anyone else, he couldn't say no to her. In those letters, we have some of the most detailed theology of Martin Luther explained in writing. And we never would have had these writings without Katie!

So people made up stories that they fell in love while they were still living as a monk and a nun, and that they ran away because they loved each other more than God.

People also published horrible things about Katie as a wife. Even those who received free things from Martin, and took things from his house, now wrote that his new wife was stingy. (But these people really only cared about money.) They said she left her vow of poverty because she was greedy.

But Luther's close friends saw the truth. Even the friends, like Melanchthon, who were against the marriage at first, quickly changed their minds and thought Katie was the best thing to happen to Martin. People couldn't just steal things from his house anymore. And Katie did not impede his ministry; she was the gasoline poured on the fire of his work.

As a result, Luther's work grew, and so did his love for Katie. He grew to trust her and her judgment completely. They were a team.

A team of two. For now.

AN UNUSUAL MARRIAGE

It didn't take long, though, before another rumor started circulating: if Katie got pregnant, she would give birth to the devil. What else, these superstitious people wondered, could come from the marriage of a fallen monk and nun?

8

Blessing of Children

1526–1552

NEITHER MARTIN nor Katie had grown up in a very loving home. Both had been sent to live at a school when they were in kindergarten. Both of them had difficult or absent relationships with their families. Martin recalled his mother beating him, leaving bruises all over because he took a walnut from the

KATIE LUTHER

pantry once when he was hungry. Katie remembered feeling abandoned and forgotten from the tender age of five, and after she escaped, her family had refused to take her back.

So when Katie gave birth to her first child, neither of them knew how to raise a loving family.

Yet the world was watching to see what kind of family Katie and Martin would have. Some people wondered if the children of this runaway nun and church troublemaker would be like demons. Other people wondered if the Luther children would be wild and undisciplined. After all, Martin Luther wrote that we are saved by faith in Christ, not from works of the law. So how would they raise their kids? How would this theology play out in an actual home with actual children?

Yet in June of 1526, when Katie gave birth to their first son, he was not the devil, just a regular baby. They named him Johannes, "Hans" for short. And as he grew up, the paradox of Christian freedom

BLESSING OF CHILDREN

that Martin wrote about and that Katie believed, continued to guide their parenting:

> A Christian is completely free, subject to nothing, and no one. A Christian is a dutiful servant, subject to everyone.

The next summer, in 1527, when Katie was already pregnant again, the bubonic plague, called the *black death*, had spread more and more and finally shut down normal life in Wittenberg. People all over Wittenberg were dying of this horrible disease. And when all the students who rented rooms from the Luthers left to go home during this outbreak, Martin and Katie decided to open up their home to use as a community hospital.

Katie was five-months pregnant and taking care of a fourteen-month-old baby as disease filled their home. All over Europe, 30–75 percent of people who caught the black death died. She tried to keep her baby on the other side of the house, while she ran that hospital with discipline and cleanliness. She and the nurses she trained (just like her aunt had trained her) kept their patients clean, gave them herbs, washed their sores with vinegar, and bandaged them up. They held the hands of dying and diseased people and prayed with them.

Then in December, right around Christmastime, with the plague still spreading throughout Wittenberg, Katie gave birth to a daughter, and they called her Elisabeth.

BLESSING OF CHILDREN

However, Elisabeth didn't make it to her first birthday. She died August 3, 1528. Martin and Katie didn't talk or write about their loss to many people. Their pain was so deep. The grief overtook them quietly, and they reached for the hope of the resurrection.

On May 4, 1529, Katie gave birth to another daughter, and they named her Magdalena (often just called "Lena") after Katie's aunt who had helped them so much. By then the plague had left Wittenberg, and Martin began traveling again. He preached all over the country, leaving Katie in charge of running the Black Cloister and taking care of their two living children. He was gone for months and months at a time. But he would write his friends in Wittenberg, asking them to go and check on Katie, and bring her gifts on his behalf.

After Martin had finished his traveling, news came that both his parents had died. So he had to leave Katie again to go help his family take care of all their things. Then in 1531, Katie gave birth to another son,

KATIE LUTHER

whom they called Martin, after his dad. Two years later, in January 1533, she gave birth to another son, Paul, named after the apostle. And in December 1534, during a hard winter, she gave birth to another girl, and they named her Margaretha, which was also a family name.

Within the first ten years of marriage, Katie had given birth to six children, and one of them had died. Their house was always busy, and everyone was watching to see how they would raise their children. Their life surely had its worries and pressures, but Katie and Martin knew to trust God for strength.

Martin Luther wrote songs for his children—some of those songs we still sing today. The family would sit around at night, singing songs of praise. Martin composed songs not just for worship, but also as a means of teaching his children life-changing truths about God. Katie would sing along too, teaching the kids different harmonies like the nuns used to sing in chapel. Though now she sang with a baby on her lap.

BLESSING OF CHILDREN

— A Mighty Fortress —

Sometime in the late 1520s, Martin Luther wrote a new hymn. But it was based on a very old text: Psalm 46. The name of the song is taken from the first words of the song. In English, the first words are "A mighty fortress is our God" (or, in German, "*Ein feste Burg ist unser Gott*"). This hymn is one of the most famous songs that Martin wrote. The first verse goes like this:

A mighty fortress is our God,
A bulwark never failing;
Our helper he, amid the flood
Of mortal ills prevailing.
For still our ancient foe
Does seek to work us woe;
His craft and power are great,
And, armed with cruel hate,
On earth is not his equal.

Martin wanted his children to be taught the basics of the Christian faith at home. He didn't believe faith was just a church thing, but an everyday family thing. So he wrote a small catechism that parents

— The Catechism —

The Apostle's Creed has three articles or parts. Luther's catechism covers all three parts. Using the catechism, a child would first memorize each article. Then the father would say "What does this mean?" and the child would give the memorized answer. The family would turn this into a game, and pretty soon, the questions and answers were a regular part of the family conversation. Here's an example of the third article, with question and answer:

III. The Third Article: On Becoming Holy:
"I believe in the Holy Spirit, the holy Christian church, the communion of the saints, the forgiveness of sins, the resurrection of the body, and the life everlasting. Amen."

BLESSING OF CHILDREN

and children could use to memorize some basic theology and talk about it together. His catechism was a simple booklet, containing simple theological questions and answers. Parents could use it to teach

Question: What does this mean?

Answer: I believe that I cannot by my own reason or strength believe in Jesus Christ, my Lord, or come to him, but the Holy Spirit has called me through the gospel, enlightened me with his gifts, and sanctified and preserved me in the true faith, just as he calls, gathers, enlightens, and sanctifies the whole Christian church on earth, and preserves it in union with Jesus Christ in the one true faith, in which Christian church he daily forgives abundantly all my sins, and the sins of all believers, and at the last day will raise me up and all the dead and will grant everlasting life to me and to all who believe in Christ. This is most certainly true.

their children at home. The topics included: The Apostle's Creed (which talks about the Trinity), the Ten Commandments, the Lord's Prayer, baptism, Communion, confession, and forgiveness.

When Katie first held *The Small Catechism* and read through it, she told Martin, "Everything in this book is about me." The catechism didn't talk about Katie, but it spoke to her so deeply it almost seemed that way. Things like learning to tell the difference between law and gospel, seeing how perfect God's law is, learning the power of God's forgiveness—all of this seeped into Katie's heart. Through *The Small Catechism*, she learned God's truth right alongside her children. It made theology practical and accessible.

Martin had also translated the Bible into German, and though Katie had recited portions of the Bible in Latin from the time she was a child, she had never read it in her own language. So Martin challenged Katie to read through it, and even offered her money if she read through the whole thing. He then joked with a friend that "my Katie now understands the

BLESSING OF CHILDREN

Psalms better than all the papists put together."
(A *papist* is someone who follows the pope.)

God was preparing Katie. All of her Bible reading
and Scripture memory would be needed, because
Katie's biggest challenges lay ahead. She would need
the encouragement of the Psalms to get through the
next season of her life.

9

Loss upon Loss

1527–1542

WHEN ANOTHER WAVE of the black death hit Wittenberg again a few years later, the Luthers' home was again transformed into a hospital. While Martin used the pulpit to keep pointing people to the resurrection, Katie felt like she was beating back death with a stick. Death became an everyday part of life. But that didn't make it any easier. If anything, it made life harder, and the longing for heaven stronger.

— Black Death —

Although people in Luther's time didn't understand what caused the black death, we now know that the bubonic plague was a bacterial disease carried by fleas who lived on rats. People who got sick would get sores all over their bodies and have high fevers. The disease first hit in the 1300s. During this time an estimated 75 million to 200 million people died. A new strain hit in the 1500s and spread all over Europe again. It's unknown how many people died during this second outbreak. With their better knowledge of health and cleanliness, deaths were much less but still in the millions, hitting the poor the hardest. In the 1800s, a third wave of black death appeared in Asia, and that is when scientists were able to find out it came from the fleas on rats. Black death can now be treated with antibiotics.

LOSS UPON LOSS

It wasn't just the plague though; other diseases invaded their home. Her husband, Martin, was getting sicker all the time. When he traveled, Katie put together packages of her handmade medicines and ointments. And she wrote him often whenever he was away, begging him to take care of himself.

If he died, how would they survive? Katie would have nothing. Her children would have nothing. The very idea of priests or monks getting married was so new that the law did not allow them to leave money for their families when they died. He needed to stay alive!

Martin would write back to her, and tell her that she was always in God's hands, and that was the safest place for her to be. He said he trusted God more than any human law to provide for her. But after a very scary sickness which almost killed him, Martin wrote a will, a document stating all of his wishes if he should die. Katie was to keep what she owned and take care of the children. He also publicly spoke out against some of the harsh treatment of widows.

89

But then one day, Katie got sick herself! She had been pregnant again, but she miscarried (which means that before the baby was born, he died inside her). This situation caused Katie to develop an infection, and as she lay in bed, her family scrambled to take care of her. All of the women she had trained as nurses took shifts caring for her.

Yet no one could bring down her fever. As she slipped from being awake to asleep all throughout the day, she would whisper Psalm 31 to herself. Over and over, as the pain overwhelmed her, she prayed: "In you, O Lord, I put my trust . . ."

Martin Luther didn't leave her bedside, but he couldn't handle seeing his wife in such pain. She was so sick that he wanted to ask God to come and take her, so she could be free from her pain. But when he looked at the eyes of his children, he knew they needed their mother. So he prayed for her to endure the sickness and come out on the other side. After almost two weeks of being in and out of consciousness, the fever broke, and Katie started to recover.

LOSS UPON LOSS

Yet she was so weak it was still a long time before she could leave her bed. She had been sick so long and lost so much strength that she had to learn to walk again. She didn't even have the strength to stand. As she got stronger, sometimes she would use furniture to hold herself up as she moved around the room. Or at other times, she would just crawl on the floor to get something.

Katie focused her strong will and determination to get better. Her husband needed her. Her children needed her. The whole household needed her. And it wasn't long until she was back running the house, and giving orders to everyone.

This tightly knit family loved each other. Martin and Katie didn't want to send their children off to boarding school, as both their families had done to them when they were kids. Instead, they provided room and board to university students in exchange for tutoring their oldest son, Hans. But he was growing up, and he soon outgrew his tutors and was ready for more academic challenges.

KATIE LUTHER

So they found a school to send him to in Torgau. When he was fourteen years old, Hans moved into a boarding school.

— In His Own Words —

Martin Luther wrote several books on the Psalms. He loved this part of God's word. In 1531 he wrote *The Summaries of the Psalms*, a book that gives an overview of every single psalm. Here is what Martin said about Psalm 31, the psalm he prayed for his beloved Katie in her sickness.

> The thirty-first Psalm is a universal psalm of thanks, a psalm of prayer, and a psalm of comfort, all at the same time. It is spoken in the person of Christ and for all his saints, who . . . are plagued their entire lives—inwardly with fears and troubles; outwardly with persecutions, slander, and contempt. Yet they are comforted and delivered by God out of all of them.

LOSS UPON LOSS

It was hard for Katie to have her family broken apart, though she was proud of her son. He was ready. She remembered all of the family separations she had to endure as a child, and she told herself this was different. Hans was not being sent away, he was growing up. She told him to write often and to tell her right away if he ever needed anything. It was the right time for Hans to be away, but she missed him deeply.

Then four weeks later tragedy struck again. Their daughter Lena became very sick. This was the daughter that God had given them after their baby daughter Elisabeth died. Martin and Katie had turned all of their quiet grief for Elisabeth into love for this new child, Lena, and they lavished grace on her and always held her close.

She was now thirteen years old. Lena was close to her parents, and Hans's best friend. She was also her mother's right hand, and her father's delight. But now she was very ill, and as much as Katie tried to nurse her to health, Lena kept getting worse. Over the last few years, Martin had been sick and almost died, but God had healed him. Katie had been sick and almost died, but God had also given her healing. So as their daughter's condition worsened and she approached death, Martin and Katie held out hope that God would heal her too. But Lena kept getting sicker. Martin wrote to the school and told them to send Hans home. Maybe Lena had become sick because she missed him and seeing him again might give her strength!

LOSS UPON LOSS

Hans arrived home and tried his best to cheer her up, but after four days of continual decline, thirteen-year-old Lena died in her father's arms. Martin Luther wept bitterly—his crying was heard all over the house. Katie stood in the corner of the room silent, with her face turned away, too stunned to cry or move. Everything screamed inside of her. *It couldn't be!* She had held the hands of many people who had died. She was around sick and dying people frequently. But this was too much.

Her world broke. And the whole family deeply mourned.

After Lena's funeral, Martin forced himself to return to his work and made Hans go back to school, even though Hans was reluctant to leave home. But Katie had nowhere to go. She was left at home, surrounded everywhere by memories of her Lena. But once again, God turned Katie's grief into a magnet for her to find other hurting people.

More children came into the Luther home, but not in the way she could have ever expected.

10

An Open Home
1525–1546

OVER THE YEARS, more than ten orphans stayed with the Luthers. Some were nieces or nephews whose parents had died. Others were children of distant relatives who had nowhere else to go. Some stayed for just a few years, and some for longer. Katie was generous with all of them.

As the orphans grew up, Martin's job was to make sure each of the children got a good job or a good marriage. But since he traveled a lot, Katie became the person in their lives who knew their favorite foods and listened to their hopes and dreams. When Martin was traveling, she would include in her letters to him if one of the children was struggling, and together, through their correspondence, the two of them would work out what to do to help the child. They arranged for some to go to school or university when the time came. Once a young pastor came around, wanting to marry

— Marriage in the 1500s —

If you lived in Germany when Martin and Katie did, you could get married pretty early. According to the law, girls were allowed to marry at age twelve and boys at age fourteen. But most of the time, they waited until they were in their late teens and early twenties.

AN OPEN HOME

one of the girls living with them. Katie listened to his sermons, and then sent him away as unfit because she did not like his doctrine. In another case, one of the girls married, but when her husband died young, she moved back into the Black Cloister. It was her home.

People would sometimes roll their eyes at how generous Katie was with the orphans in her care. In preparation for one of the girls' weddings, Katie sewed beautiful gold thread cords onto her wedding dress. Some thought it was too beautiful for an orphan to wear, especially an orphan who had not always been very well behaved for Martin and Katie. But generosity with the least was a principle in the Luther household. It was what living out freedom looked like. It was what understanding the depths of God's love looked like.

And Katie's generosity grew. She and Martin opened their home even wider. During the Reformation, Martin became so famous that kings and queens all over Europe were discussing his writings, and whole governments began to change. Many of these royals and nobles would travel to Wittenberg with the plan

AN OPEN HOME

of staying with the Luther family. (It was considered the highest honor to have a king or queen visit your house!) However, due to Martin and Katie's generosity, the Luther home also started to get a reputation.

When Prince George of Anhalt decided to visit the Luthers' home, a friend who had previously visited, advised him not to go. The Black Cloister, he said, was "the lodging place of a motley group of young people, students, girls, widows, old women, and quite young boys." In other words, the home was loud and boisterous! Royals started deciding that if they wanted to visit Martin Luther, they would prefer to stay somewhere a bit quieter.

Even Martin and Katie sometimes wanted to escape the Black Cloister and all of its noise. In time, they were able to buy Katie's early childhood home and farm in Zuhlsdorf that Katie's brother had inherited but no longer wanted. The home was really rundown, but that didn't bother Katie. The elector near the farm was a friend of the Luthers, and he offered to help fix the place up, even supplying lumber.

This small home in Zuhlsdorf became a sanctuary for the Luther family. As the number of guests at the Black Cloister grew, the new farmland provided more crops to help feed the crowds living there. And as the hosts of the Black Cloister grew older, the new home created a retreat for the family when they needed more quiet.

For even as the demands upon Martin and Katie increased, their own strength was starting to decline.

— Would You Pay for Wood? —

When Martin and Katie lived in Germany, wooden boards and planks were expensive. Each one had to be cut by hand using axes and saws. One shopping list says that a mattress cost two coins while three boards cost twice that much!

11

The Aftermath
1546

IN THE CHILL of winter, nothing was growing in the garden. Once again, Martin Luther was called away to travel back to his hometown, but his sickness kept dragging him down. Katie didn't think her husband was well enough to travel. Walking was even becoming difficult. So Martin asked her for another packet of her homemade medicines and ointments. Katie sent their sons, Hans, Martin, and Paul, with him to bring his medicines, make sure that their dad was taking the medicines, look after him, and be a good help.

Katie kept writing to Martin, though, telling him how worried she was about his health.

He replied to her on February 10, 1546. His letter started off: "To the holy lady, full of worries, Mrs. Katharina Luther, doctor, the lady of Zuhlsdorf, at Wittenberg, my gracious and dear mistress of the house . . ."

Martin then wrote a really funny story saying that her worries were creating all of these almost-disasters. He joked that every time she worried, rocks fell out of the sky, and he had to dodge them. Later he knew she was worrying again, because his room had caught fire, a whole building had gone up in flames, and he barely made it out alive. He joked that these made-up disasters were happening one after the other, and that he barely survived with all of the rocks falling from

— In Their Own Words —

Martin Luther loved to say funny things. He had a huge sense of humor. Here's part of the actual letter he wrote to Katie when she was worrying about him.

> We thank you in a most friendly way for your great concern, because of which you could not sleep. For since that time that you have worried about us, fire wanted to consume us in our accommodations, right up to the door of my room. And yesterday— doubtless because of the power of your concern—a stone would have struck us on the head and crushed us like a mouse. For in our apartment for two days limestone crumbled down over our head until we called some people who took hold of the stone with two fingers. A piece as long as a long cushion and a large hand wide fell out.

KATIE LUTHER

THE AFTERMATH

the sky and their rooms catching on fire. Then he said, "I worry that if you do not stop worrying the earth will finally swallow us up and all the elements will chase us. . . . Pray, and let God worry. You have certainly not been commanded to worry about me or yourself. 'Cast your burden on the LORD, and he will sustain you' [Ps. 55:22]." He wanted her to know that of all the things that can hurt us, worry is at the top.

Despite all his joking, Martin was, in fact, very sick.

Eight days later, three of Luther's friends who had been traveling with him and their boys returned to the Black Cloister. Katie was outside early in the morning. She could see her breath as she was doing chores when she saw them walking toward her without Martin. Her blood chilled, and she cried out as she knew what had happened before any of them opened their mouths. Martin Luther had died.

Katie would hold onto that last letter from Martin. She clung to his words: "You have certainly not been commanded to worry about me or yourself. 'Cast your burden on the LORD, and he will sustain

KATIE LUTHER

you' [Ps. 55:22]." Katie did worry, though—especially for her children. With her husband gone, the law said that she had no right to the Black Cloister, to any of her gardens, her old family property in Zuhlsdorf, her farm animals, or even her children. In one day, her life completely changed.

But Martin Luther had written a will. He didn't trust lawyers, maybe because he had trained to be one. When he wrote his will, he knew that it was only valid if lawyers signed that they witnessed him signing it. However, since he didn't want to involve lawyers, he decided to have his friends, who were professors at the Wittenberg University, witness him sign his will. He figured theology professors would be considered more reliable than lawyers. He wanted to make sure his family was taken care of.

Martin had written particular things in his will in regard to his wife, Katie. For their whole marriage, Katie had run the house, directed the finances, expanded their domain, cared for the sick and anyone who came to their doorstep, all while she also

108

THE AFTERMATH

supported Martin's ministry. So although the law required that women had a male guardian, Martin thought the very idea of Katie needing a guardian was hilarious. Instead, he wrote in his will that Katie was to be her own guardian and the children's guardian. She could easily and capably manage herself and her own money, decisions, and property. He wanted the freedom she had enjoyed in their marriage to continue after his death.

He had meant well, but what he was suggesting was illegal. The fact that his will was not witnessed by lawyers and that it requested things that were illegal (like Katie being her own guardian) meant that the death of Martin Luther forced Katie to spend her time fighting to keep her children. Even while she was mourning the loss of her husband, she battled to not lose her children too.

For the first few weeks, Luther's friends looked after her and loaned her money when she needed it. When he was alive, Martin Luther had asked his friend, Elector Johann Frederick, (who was like a governor of that territory) to take responsibility for Katie. Being a busy man, the elector assigned Chancellor Brück to sort out Luther's will. But this chancellor didn't like Katie at all. Once, he had gone to Luther's house to ask for help with a political decision. He had seen Martin Luther first talk the situation over with Katie and then decide to stay out of the chancellor's political battle.

So the chancellor had held a longtime grudge against Katie. And he felt Martin had been far too generous with her. Now the chancellor said Katie didn't need a big home, all of these farm animals, servants, or even her children. She should just relax. She should live a quiet, small life now, he said, with maybe just her daughter to keep her company. Her oldest son was at a university. But her younger two boys should be placed in boarding schools, so they wouldn't be too influenced by their mother.

The tight-knit Luther family huddled together. Katie knew that if she threw a tantrum and demanded to keep her children and her home, people would just

THE AFTERMATH

think she was an irrational woman and not listen. Instead of seeing her as gentle, quiet, and meek, they'd imagine she was demanding, loud, and entitled—the kind of woman who couldn't be trusted with children or a household. Katie had to work this problem out with wisdom and patience.

The elector thought of another plan to help. He asked if any of Luther's friends would like to take guardianship of Katie, so that she could go back to her life as usual. However, this idea was met with an immediate no from all of his friends, as they all knew personally that Katie had a strong personality. Their own wives were gentle and obedient, and if they allowed this strong-willed woman to do things that even their wives didn't do, what would that do to the peace in their own homes?

Since no one wanted to be guardian over Katie, the elector appointed a group of men to try to keep an eye on her. For this group, he selected Katie's brother Hans von Bora, as well as Erasmus Spiegel, who was the captain of the city guard. Then he named Martin

111

Luther's brother, Jacob, along with a doctor from Wittenberg and the mayor of Wittenberg to be the children's guardians.

If Katie was going to keep her family together, she would have to convince both the group of men in charge of her and the group of men in charge of her children that keeping her family together was a good idea.

She came up with a plan. Although they had lived in the Black Cloister, this building had never belonged to Martin Luther. The elector had just let Martin stay and run the place after the monks left. Her children would need a good house and property they could own and inherit when they grew up. So she worked with all the guardians and wrote letters asking for help from anyone she knew. Once she had collected enough money, she got permission to buy a small estate called "Wachsdorf" that her children would inherit when she died. That way, they'd always have a home in case the large Black Cloister wasn't available to them.

THE AFTERMATH

Once the problem of a permanent home was settled, she was able to convince her children's guardians, one at a time, that it would be best if her children lived with her. Finally, Elector Frederick even let them continue to use the Black Cloister. She would still have to take care of all of the Wittenberg University students who lived there, but no one could seem to manage that household as well as Katie. At last, it was all settled. Katie had her children, her home, and her farm.

However, just a few months after Katie finally got everything settled, and had all her children home with her, she faced another battle. War came to Wittenberg.

12

War in Wittenberg

1546–1552

WITTENBERG HAD BECOME a military zone. The Holy Roman Empire now had two kinds of electors. Some were Protestant, like the one who had protected Martin Luther, and some were Roman Catholic, loyal to the pope. The Protestant electors called themselves the Schmalkaldic League, and before long they saw themselves as a replacement for the Holy Roman Empire. After all, the emperor was only the emperor because he'd been crowned by the pope. That made the Schmalkaldic League a threat to the authority of the emperor. So Emperor Charles V fought back, and he sent his troops marching toward Wittenberg.

Katie and her children packed a wagon with whatever valuables they could fit, and fled with other

— What Was the Schmalkaldic League? —

The Schmalkaldic League was like a team of rulers (known as electors) in Germany during the 1500s. They joined together to defend their rights and beliefs as Reformers who followed Martin Luther. This league started in 1532, but began to fall apart after losing a big battle in 1547. It took almost a decade for the league to finally reach a victory and bring peace to their lands. (This is known as the Peace of Augsburg.)

refugees to Magdeburg, a city about 50 miles away. They spent the winter there away from the battle.

Months later, they heard it was safe to return to the Black Cloister. So they drove the wagon and all their things back. But as they returned to Wittenberg, they noticed that Katie's gardens, farms, and all of her livestock had been destroyed. She could return to her work at the Black Cloister, but she would have no food to serve the students living there.

Immediately, she began to rebuild what was lost with the help of Elector Johann Frederick. But before she could accomplish much, Emperor Charles V's armies attacked Wittenberg again. Katie and her children fled the city just barely in time. But Elector Johann Frederick did not. He was captured. No longer would he be able to protect Katie and her family.

She was once again a war refugee. And now without the elector protecting her, Katie had to think of solutions fast. Where would she stay? How would she live? It wasn't just her survival, but her children's survival on the line. Their legal guardians couldn't

KATIE LUTHER

help; they were all scattered by war. Some friends were close by, but they had no power to protect her.

So she took out her pen and wrote to a powerful, old friend of hers—King Christian III in Denmark. They had become friends back before her marriage when she lived with the Cranach family. He told her then that she should never hesitate to ask for help. So she asked for safe refuge in his country.

The king not only sent her money, but also told her he'd provide a safe place for her family to stay in Denmark, if she could just make it there. She and her kids started their trip, but they were refugees moving through an area with soldiers and battles everywhere. Travel was very dangerous. They made it as far as Braunschweig, but it was too dangerous to go further.

Then, on June of 1547, she received word that she didn't have to go to Denmark after all! Her friends wrote that Wittenberg was safe again. She could come home to the Black Cloister. They said her home was untouched. Excitedly, she brought her kids back to

WAR IN WITTENBERG

Wittenberg, only to find that her farms, land, and everything outside of the city limits were destroyed yet again.

So with no elector to give the money he had promised, Katie was living in poverty. She wrote letters to all of Luther's old friends, asking for help. Her children needed food. She begged for help from everyone she could think of.

The only one who helped with an open hand was once again her own friend, King Christian III, who sent her money regularly. It wasn't enough to live on,

— Friends in High Places —

King Christian III was an important king in Denmark during the lifetime of the Luthers. The country of Denmark lies on the north side of Germany. King Christian III ruled from 1534 to 1559. During his reign, he changed the main religion of his country from Catholicism to Lutheranism. King Christian III also made the government stronger and changed how things were run in Denmark.

KATIE LUTHER

WAR IN WITTENBERG

but it always helped. Luther's powerful friends retreated from her. They complained that she must not know how to handle money, otherwise she wouldn't be asking them for help so much. Nothing could be further from the truth.

Through all the pain and poverty, Katie kept writing to the person who actually treated her as a friend, King Christian III. In one letter she wrote: "More damage has been done to me by my friends than by my enemies. For these and other reasons, I am compelled to humbly petition Your Royal Highness to help me since everybody treats me like a stranger and no one has mercy on me."

Through the king's kindness, Katie had received help and wanted to do the same for others. So she kept the Black Cloister open and hosted university students to the best of her ability. But in 1552, the black death, that horrible disease, invaded Wittenberg again. Without Martin and money, Katie knew she couldn't open a hospital again. She could no longer afford nurses or medicine or food.

KATIE LUTHER

Now all she could do was try to protect her children. The older children, Hans and Martin, were away, studying at universities. So she took Paul and Margaretha, and together they loaded a cart to flee to Torgau, 40 miles away.

But on the way, as Katie drove, something suddenly startled the horses. The cart lurched and rocked. As it was about to tip over, Katie jumped off. As she landed in a ditch filled with cold water, she hit her head hard on a rock and became paralyzed.

Her children struggled to pull their mother out of the water and get her back onto the cart. It took a long time, but they finally got her to Torgau, found a place to stay, and located a doctor to help her. Katie was very sick. She lay in bed for three months. Her children hoped she would regain strength, but her body was too weak.

On December 20, 1552, she finally found rest in the arms of her Savior, and her faith became sight.

She was buried at St. Mary's Church in Torgau, Germany, and Luther's friend, Melanchthon, wrote

WAR IN WITTENBERG

her obituary and sent out invitations to her funeral the next day. A surprisingly large crowd came of university professors and students who knew her and people she had served even in her own poverty.

Katharina von Bora Luther went by many names. She was called "the mother of the Reformation" and "the morning star of Wittenberg."

But Katie saw her life as a collection of ordinary days, filled with ordinary chores, serving ordinary people. Her ordinary days included cleaning rooms, cooking food, doing dishes, weeding the garden, comforting the sick, making clothes for the orphans in her care, and teaching them the miracle of the ordinary life, given to them in Christ Jesus.

She didn't have to try to be extra holy or earn God's favor. Because of salvation by faith alone, she was free to just be. She was free from the expectations others had of her. She was free from people-pleasing and earning her way to love. She was fully loved on account of Christ alone. So she devoted her life to love others the way Christ loved her.

Conclusion

Lessons from a Life

WE KNOW THE BIBLE talks about the importance of doing good works and following God, and it also talks about Jesus coming to die for our sins. The relationship between Jesus dying on the cross and our good works is important to know because getting it wrong can cause a lot of heartache.

Martin Luther divided Scripture into two main

CONCLUSION

categories: law and gospel. The law was anything in the Old or New Testaments where God told his people to do or not do something. The gospel is Jesus fulfilling the law for us, on our behalf. In other words, the law shows us our sin, and the gospel shows us our Savior.

But throughout history, people have used God's law to manipulate others for selfish gain. Or people turn the Bible into just a rulebook that gets you to heaven. The gospel isn't useful for gaining power in this world, or power over other people.

Even when the apostle Paul so richly described the gospel, people started to wonder: If the gospel really went that deep, and covered and redeemed that much, then what motivation would anyone have to do good works (Romans 6)?

In *The Freedom of the Christian*, Martin Luther wrote about freedom found in grace being a more powerful motivator for good works then the law. Why? Because the law was just us trying to be good so God would love us. The gospel was God's goodness overpowering us and taking over.

CONCLUSION

This teaching on freedom is what transformed Katie Luther's life, and gave her courage to live her life with her eyes fixed on Jesus and her hands serving her neighbors. It helped her release the life handed to her where she had to earn her righteousness. It gave her freedom to use her gifts without fear. It helped her withstand criticism from many people who were uncomfortable with her choices—as her identity and righteousness were secure in Christ's death and resurrection.

In this teaching of Christian freedom, sin isn't just something we do or don't do. Instead, sin is a trap we are caught in, oppressing us, that we need freedom from. One of the biggest sins each of us needs to address is self-righteousness, meaning our feeling that if we are just good enough, we won't need Jesus. If we just impress God enough, then Jesus wouldn't have needed to die. These good works just mask a heart wanting to push God away and save ourselves.

The gospel frees us from this trap and says that Jesus paid it all.

CONCLUSION

There's nothing left for us to do to please God. But now that we belong to God, not to the trap of sin, what should we do?

We should love our neighbors because that's what God's family does. We get to be the hands and feet of Jesus, not so he'll love us, but because we belong to him, and he already considers us his treasure. It's from the certainty of his love that we can do anything without the burden of self-righteousness, anxiety, or fear.

Study Questions

Chapter 1: The Escape

1. Why did Katharina von Bora and the other nuns decide to escape the cloister? Why was Easter Sunday a smart choice for the nuns to escape?

2. What had the nuns been taught about achieving perfection and gaining God's favor? How did Martin Luther's teachings challenge these beliefs?

3. Why did Martin Luther believe that monks and nuns who had been forced to take vows did not have to keep them? What did Martin Luther teach about the freedom of all Christians?

STUDY QUESTIONS

Chapter 2: A Life without Freedom

1. Describe Katie von Bora's early life. What challenges did she face after her mother's death, and how did those challenges shape her future?

2. What was *The Rule of Saint Benedict*, and how did it influence the way of life for Katie and the other girls at the cloister?

3. How did things change for Katie when she moved to the convent in Nimbschen? How was the cloister different from the one in Brehna?

Chapter 3: Life as a Nun

1. Explain the three vows that Katie had to follow as a nun: obedience, poverty, and chastity. What was Katie's life like because of these vows?

2. What was a relic? How did the nuns use relics? Why did people donate relics?

3. Describe the intense prayer schedule that Katie and the other nuns followed. Why was prayer so important

STUDY QUESTIONS

to them? What other chores did they also have to do every day?

Chapter 4: Reformation Rumblings

1. What things were wrong in the church during the time of Martin Luther? What were indulgences? How did the church use them to raise money? What did Martin Luther's *Ninety-Five Theses* say about these things that were wrong in the church?

2. How did Martin Luther's writings and ideas become known to so many people? Martin Luther taught that salvation is by grace through faith. How was that different from what the church at that time was teaching?

3. Explain the concept of paradox using the example from Martin Luther's writing, *The Freedom of the Christian*. How can someone be both free and a servant at the same time?

4. How did Martin Luther's teaching change what Katie thought about being a nun? What made her think God might have a different purpose for her?

STUDY QUESTIONS

Chapter 5: Falling in Love

1. Why was it more difficult for the nuns to leave their vows compared to the monks? What laws and customs made it harder for women of that time?

2. Describe Katie's relationship with Jerome Baumgärtner and her decision to wait for him. Why did Jerome never come back? Why did Katie refuse to marry Caspar Glatz?

3. Why did some people gossip about Katie during this time of her life, and how did her reputation suffer as a result?

Chapter 6: Marriage before Love

1. How did it happen that Martin Luther finally proposed to Katie? How did his sense of Christian duty and commitment to helping others play a role in his decision?

2. Describe the attitude and feelings Martin and Katie had toward each other on their wedding day. How did their feelings for one another grow and change over time?

3. What early challenges did Katie face as she moved into the Black Cloister after marrying Martin Luther? How would you describe her approach to these challenges?

STUDY QUESTIONS

Chapter 7: An Unusual Marriage

1. How was Martin and Katie's partnership an unusual marriage for their time? How was their marriage an example of cooperation and mutual respect?

2. How did Martin and Katie's strong wills work together to make them good partners?

3. How did Katie encourage Martin to respond to theological debates? How did she help him to write some of his important writings?

Chapter 8: Blessing of Children

1. How did Martin and Katie create a loving family environment for their children? Do you think Martin's time as a monk or Katie's time as a nun helped them teach their children about Jesus?

2. Why do you think Martin's hymn "A Mighty Fortress Is Our God" is still famous today? How did music play a role in the Luther family?

3. What is a catechism? What was Katie's reaction to *The Small Catechism*? How did it help her understand

STUDY QUESTIONS

theology better? How did it help her be a better mother?

Chapter 9: Loss upon Loss

1. How did the recurring outbreaks of the bubonic plague (black death) affect the Luthers, their household, their town, and their country? How did Martin and Katie respond to the constant presence of death and disease in their community?

2. Describe the family's reaction to repeated sorrow and loss. How did these painful events deepen their faith and reliance on God's providence? In what practical ways did Martin and Katie cope with their losses?

Chapter 10: An Open Home

1. What was the Luther family's approach to hospitality and generosity? How can we follow their examples in our own lives?

2. How did the Luthers' hospitality and generosity show what they believed and what was most important to them?

STUDY QUESTIONS

Chapter 11: The Aftermath

1. In Martin's last letter to Katie before his death, how did he use humor to address her worries? What message was he trying to convey to her through his playful storytelling?

2. Because of the laws and customs of Katie's time, what challenges did she face after Martin's death? What problems with Martin's will made it illegal?

3. How did the Black Cloister become the way for Katie to keep her family together? Why was the Black Cloister especially important to her?

Chapter 12: War in Wittenberg

1. What happened to Katie's property and livelihood because of the war? How did the destruction of her farms and land affect her ability to support herself and her children?

2. How did the doctrine of "salvation by faith alone" make a difference in Katie's everyday tasks and relationships?

3. How can Katie's life be an example to people today?

STUDY QUESTIONS

4. In what ways did Katie's life challenge traditional roles and expectations for women of her time? What kind of things did Katie do to keep the spread of the gospel and the well-being of her family her first priorities?

Conclusion: Lessons from a Life

1. How is sin not only wrong actions but also a trap that imprisons us? How does recognizing this perspective on sin help your understanding of freedom and grace?

2. What lessons learned from Katie Luther's life can be applied to your own life today? How can you embrace the freedom of God's grace while still pursuing acts of love and service to others?

Timeline

KATHARINA VON BORA LUTHER'S LIFE AND WORLD EVENTS

Year	Events	Age
1450	The printing press with moveable type is invented by Johannes Gutenberg.	
1483	Martin Luther is born on November 10.	
1499	Katharina von Bora is born on January 29.	0
1504	Katie moves to cloister school in Brehna, Germany.	5
1505	The pope commissions the rebuilding of St. Peter's Basilica in Rome.	6
1508	Katie is brought to the convent in Nimbschen, Germany.	9
1515	On October 8, Katie takes vows to become a nun.	16

KATIE'S LIFE   WORLD EVENTS

TIMELINE

Year	Events	Age
1517	Martin Luther posts his *Ninety-Five Theses* on October 31.	18
1520	Martin Luther publishes *The Freedom of the Christian*.	21
1521	Philip Melanchthon, Luther's friend and co-laborer, writes *Loci Communes*, which sets the foundation for Lutheran theology.	22
1522	Martin Luther finishes translating the New Testament into German.	23
1523	In April, Katie escapes from the Nimbschen convent.	24
1524–1525	The Peasants' War. Peasants revolted against the working class in what is now Germany. The peasants lost the war, but it helped shape the rights of peasants.	25–26
1525	On June 13, Katie von Bora marries Martin Luther.	26
1526	Hans is born in June.	27
1526	In the autumn, the black death hits Wittenberg.	27
1527	Elisabeth is born in December.	28
1528	Their daughter Elisabeth dies in August.	29
1529	Magdalena is born in May.	30
1530	The Augsburg Confession is presented to Emperor Charles V outlining the key beliefs and teachings of the Lutheran faith, laying a foundation for Protestant doctrine.	31

TIMELINE

Year	Events	Age
1530	King Henry VIII of England wants to divorce his wife, Catherine, but the pope denies him. The king then uses Martin Luther's renouncing of the pope's authority as an excuse to divorce his wife anyway, breaking England off from the Roman Catholic Church.	31
1531	Martin, their son, is born in November.	32
1533	Paul is born in January.	34
1533	John Calvin converts to Protestantism through the teachings of Martin Luther.	34
1534	Martin Luther publishes the German Bible, making the Bible available to common people. Margaretha is born in December.	35
1536	John Calvin publishes *Institutes of the Christian Religion*, laying a foundation for Reformed theology.	37
1539	In the autumn, the black death hits Wittenberg again.	40
1540	Katie almost dies from a miscarriage.	41
1542	On September 20, their daughter Magdalena dies.	43
1546	Martin Luther dies on February 18. Katie and her children flee Wittenberg in November.	47
1546–1547	Schmalkaldic War breaks out and Charles V fights against the Protestant electors in the Holy Roman Empire.	47–48

TIMELINE

Year	Events	Age
1547	Katie and her children return to Wittenberg in March. In late spring, Katie and her children flee Wittenberg again. And in November, Katie and her children again return to Wittenberg.	48
1548– 1552	Katie faces poverty and lawsuits in Wittenberg.	49– 53
1549	Thomas Cranmer writes the *Book of Common Prayer* in England, establishing order of worship and prayers for the Church of England during the English Reformation.	50
1552	In the summer, the black death hits Wittenberg again.	53
1552	In September, Katie is injured on the road to Torgau. And on December 20, Katharina von Bora Luther dies.	53
1555	The Peace of Augsburg treaty is eventually signed after the Schmalkaldic War, allowing each elector to decide whether or not his region would be Roman Catholic or Protestant.	
1558	After many wars between Protestants and Roman Catholics in England, King Henry VIII's daughter Elizabeth I becomes queen of England, and establishes England firmly as a Protestant nation.	

More to Explore

IF YOU'D LIKE TO READ MORE about Katie Luther, there are several books that tell the story of her life. Some of the books in the list below are written for young readers like you. Some of the adult books in the list are challenging to read but worth the effort.

BOOKS TO TRY NEXT

Katie Luther: Mother of the Reformation by Susan Leigh (Concordia, 2016). This book is a graphic novel.

Katharine von Bora: The Morning Star of Wittenberg by Jenna Strackbein and Shanna Strackbein (Unbroken Faith, 2017). This one is a children's picture book.

MORE TO EXPLORE

ADULT BOOKS YOU MIGHT ENJOY

Katharina and Martin Luther: The Radical Marriage of a Runaway Nun and a Renegade Monk **by Michelle DeRusha (Baker, 2018).** This well-researched book describes important details about the historical and cultural context where the Luthers lived, as it focuses on the unconventional marriage of Martin and Katie Luther.

The Mother of the Reformation **by Ernst Kroker and translated by Mark E. DeGarmeaux (Concordia, 2013).** Translated from German into English, this book has a lot of exact details of dates, people, and places surrounding Katie's life. It is considered the gold standard of authoritative biographies of Katie.

Also Available from the Lives of Faith and Grace Series

Perfect for summer reading—or all year round—the Lives of Faith and Grace series will engage kids ages 8–13 with the real-life stories of Christian men and women from history. These short and lively biographies feature pencil sketch illustrations, maps, timelines, bonus sidebars, study questions, and options for further reading.

For more information, visit **crossway.org**.